My Words and Thoughts

My Words and Thoughts

Maria Vincent

authorHOUSE®

AuthorHouse™ UK
1663 Liberty Drive
Bloomington, IN 47403   USA
www.authorhouse.co.uk
Phone: 0800.197.4150

Published by AuthorHouse 10/20/2015

ISBN: 978-1-5049-4611-7 (sc)
ISBN: 978-1-5049-4612-4 (e)

Print information available on the last page.

This book is printed on acid-free paper.

For Papa, Amma, and Rose, who have helped me in every area of my growth and progress, who have never let me down, and who have always kept their faith that I can do it!

Preface

This book simply stands for who I am – a young teenager who loves to explore the world around her, spends a lot of time thinking about it and jots it down, and then tries to speak her mind to a larger public.

I started writing since I first learnt how to frame sentences. I started with little stories, and I went on to write poetry at around the age of seven. Then my writing grew into articles and essays.

This book comprises my personal views. This is a collection of my works dating back to perhaps eighth grade, but my ideas and opinions havent changed much during that time.

Compiling everything and drawing the perfect illusrations wasn't an easy task, butI enjoyed every moment of preparing this book, and I hope you'll find this book refreshing as well.

As mentioned earlier, this book is my brainchild. I wrote this book because I want to let the world know what I, as a gobal citizen, think of the many things mentioned in this book; I thus practice my freedom of speech. I don't intend to point at anyone or anything in partcular, and neither do I wish to propogate my ideas or make you believe what you feel isn't right. In the end, your opinions matter the most.

To all the readers, I would like to say this book is a collection of thoughts rather than information. It is what my mind speaks and what I guess should happen. I do want to bring into light some issues that are ignored and help society think over them. I sincerely hope that this book can bring light to you, and that I may serve society with my pen.

Happy reading!

Acknowledgements

The Almighty, for his unconditional love and blessings that have helped me come to this level.

My Mother, Rexy, for bringing literature closer to me, for the lovely stories you told, and for guiding me to be a good writer.

My Father, Vincent, for being a supporter during my every venture.

My Sister, Rose, for being the awesome buddy and a commentator who points out my mistakes, punches me, and makes me think differently.

My Teachers and Mentors for teaching me everything from ABC and 123 to complex vocabulary, maps, and equations. You played an important role in making me who I am.

My School, The Indian High School, Dubai, for the many opportunities I have received that helped me in a holistic progress.

Gulf News, for creating the space where I got the first taste of getting articles published, and for showing me how always I can better myself as a writer.

AuthorHouse, for helping me to publish my first book.

My home, The United Arab Emirates, for giving multitudinous opportunities to explore, learn, and grow, and for being a subject in my works.

My country, India, for giving me life, for giving me ideas for many of my works, and for showing me how diverse nature and lifestyles can be.

Introduction

The world around us is not the same from moment to moment; there is always a new happening. Some of these happenings are significant, and some are not. Some are so significant that we easily forget their presence, and some may be so insignificant that we might underestimate it and still try to find a story behind it.

This book mainly deals with my take on trending topics – an issue, a happening, or something I have observed and would like to think about.

This piece of nonfiction is divided into two: My Articles and Essays, and My Poems. 'My Articles and Essays' include a collection of articles based on some current issues, as well as some topics that have a vast scope for reflection, such as media and the various dimensions of progress. Many of these articles were published in the local daily, and some of them were school assignments, but they reflect my personal views.

'My Poems' is an anthology of various poems, most of them written on a lighter note. Much of the seemingly insignificant incidents have been brought to light into this section. Mainly the poems written in free verse, they stand as a testimony to my imagination and creativity, which likes to take a different step outside tradition.

This book can be enjoyed by people of all ages, and every piece of writing has a new message to reveal.

My Articles & Essays

Man's Greed

Why is man destroying his own home?

In the year 2030, a team of zoologists and botanists were roaming around in an unknown forest. Mr Felix Aglarius, a leading botanist from Spain, warned the team, "Be careful. Do not dirty or poison the catrocaphasis, the newly discovered plant. It will make the animal unconscious for two hours, but it will not have any effects on their health, if not harmed. Once the plant is harmed, it will have a fatal effect on the animals, as per our study."

"Yes, Mr Aglarius, you're right," said Clara Jones, the head of the Department of Zoology at Ohio University. The group of six proceeded, collecting the green-blue, straw-like plants along the way. The aim of this expedition was to study the strange plants and their effects on the animal world.

The group of six came across a sleeping elephant. Eric gave it the catrocaphasis. Unfortunately, Eric gave it a harmed one, and the elephant died instantly. Mr. Aglarius cried, "Eric, what have you done? You have just killed an endangered animal and broken the law. The punishment for this will have to be borne by all of us. Let's leave this place before anyone finds out."

The research team left, but without anyone's knowledge, Eric stayed back. He was greedy, and he cut off the tusks of the dead elephant. While holding them in his hand, he said, "Thanks to the vinegar, the elephant is dead. I'm rich!"

Now, do you think this is right? Of course not. Man's greed for wealth is solely responsible for the endangerment and extinction of many species, which causes nature imbalance. As it is said, everything that goes around comes around. Man will pay for destruction with his life.

How Global Warming Rules the World

Why are we setting our own home ablaze?

When people think of Kerala, a state in the southern part of India, they think of the lovely, wet, and cool weather with many coconut trees, lagoons, and backwaters – a typical coastal climate. But when I went there once, the mercury had soared up so rapidly that it was extremely hot. People here say, "Kerala is not like before. It is really hot, and the weather is changing from tolerable to intolerable."

What has caused this climate change? Most of us have read in our science textbooks that it is the abnormal heating of the earth's atmosphere. Global warming is a phenomenon that takes place due to an increase in the concentration of carbon dioxide in the atmosphere. Pollution of the air by industries, vehicles, and more contributes to the pollution of the earth's atmosphere.

Global warming, a companion of the greenhouse effect, has been an issue that has not stopped at national boundaries. Whether north, south, east, or west, global warming is one of man's worst gifts to Mother Earth.

The rise in temperature, expansion of water bodies, the death of incredible species, the disappearance of lands – we know it all. But why don't we care about such things? When we have a bad and tyrannical ruler in our country, we struggle to overthrow him and his government. Have we even lifted a finger to save the world from destruction under the rule of Global Warming the Great? Have we thought about how to overthrow his brother, Carbon Dioxide the Wicked?

Think of a baby in the heart of the Sahara. This could be the living conditions of a subtropical region like the United States in the year 2050 if we don't care about it now. So act wisely, and let's go zero on CO_2.

Preserving the Ozone Layer

What is happening to our protective armour?

Ozone is a natural gas that is found in two different layers of the atmosphere. In the upper layer, ozone protects life on earth by absorbing some of the sun's UV rays. Too many UV rays can cause skin cancer and will also harm all plants and animals.

Every year on 16 September, we celebrate International Day for the Preservation of the Ozone layer. But the ozone layer is on the verge of being destroyed due to the excessive use of chlorofluorocarbons (CFC) and other chemicals. It's not enough that the United Nations calls for action at a global level. We need to think about how our actions can help in the preservation of this lifesaving layer, which indeed can be protected through small steps. But first, the general public needs to become aware of it.

If you stop using aerosols, hairsprays, and refrigerator coolants containing CFCs, then the deterioration of our ozone can be avoided.

Haunted Experience of an Earthquake

Experiencing a natural disaster

It was a Tuesday afternoon at home after a nice, warm school day. My sister and I were having lunch, and my mom was talking on the phone when she observed that the leaves of our indoor money plant were shaking. We made funny comments about whether something was haunting the place. I stood barefoot and felt the floor trembling underneath. When I sat back in my chair, it shook as well. I shouted, "It's an earthquake!"

My sister got scared. We opened the front door, and my mother spotted the pendulum of our grandfather clock swinging rapidly. Our neighbours were out in the corridor. We had one thing to say: "It's shaking, it's shaking!" The tremors began at around 2.50 p.m. and lasted for about twenty seconds.

An earthquake of a large magnitude was triggered at the Iran-Pakistan border. Besides Dubai, Abu Dhabi, and Sharjah, the northern half of India also intensely felt the tremors. Ahmedabad, Delhi, and Chattisgarh saw many people running out to the streets from their homes and workplaces. UAE also had chaos, confusion, and fright. The earthquake was magnitude 7.8 near the epicentre.

My Culture and Your Culture
for a Better Tomorrow

Everyone's culture can change the future

Every nation, every province, and every town on this earth has its own culture. The traditions and lifestyle, as well as the wisdom and moral code of conduct of the people living in every nook and corner, have a great role to play in creating a better tomorrow.

Men across the earth often have misunderstandings between their respective cultures and traditions, which often lead to civil strife, conflict, and wars. But if these cultures are well understood, it will lead to a better tomorrow.

It is rightly emphasized that the future depends on what we do today. Whatever we do represents our culture. Culture also includes the outlook, attitudes, and goals of society. Every culture has its own pros and cons. But if the golden points of each society are highlighted and are ready to be combined, then the world will be more than peaceful, prosperous, happy, and grateful to each of its citizens.

I believe that my culture forms the basic foundation on which I build my life, using all the intellectual thoughts and facts I have gained. Wherever I live, wherever I am brought up, and whosoever are my friends, I can never live without this culture which my country has granted me through my parents. I strongly adhere to the fact that the Indian culture I follow has the power to create a better future for the world. It teaches me a lot, and I can never get a better list of moral values.

My culture teaches me to meet everybody with a smile. Nobody can deny the fact that a smile can brighten up your and your neighbour's day. Mother Teresa has rightly said, "Peace begins with a smile."

My culture advises me to live life with a sense of brotherhood. How can a nation survive without the bonds of brotherhood between each of its citizens? Without brotherhood, the country will gradually crumble. Without brotherhood, nobody can live in peace.

My culture teaches me to treat my parents, teachers, and guests in the same way as I respect and love God. Parents and teachers are the images of God who have been born on earth to show us the right path, to help us when we are in need, and to impart wisdom and the knowledge of what is right and wrong in order to lead a fruitful life. As my culture says, I believe that guests are the human forms of God, who has come to relax with us and spend some friendly and loving moments with us, lifting high our spirits. Carrying these ideals in our hearts will help us to cherish every moment of our lives. When we respect those whom we know, we will learn to respect and acknowledge our fellow men.

My culture teaches me to share the fruits of knowledge and wisdom, the gems of love and peace, and the crops of joy, happiness, and fulfillment. These things are essential to lead a life that we won't regret and to have moments that will make us happy. Through this attitude of sharing, we can spread good values across the continents and oceans.

Most important, my culture has taught me to respect everybody's views. By respecting each other's cultures, not only will we learn more about others, but we will also show that our cultures have taught us to respect others.

Such principles and values from all over the world encourage people to live in harmony with their neighbourhood and their spiritual identities. There is a link between people, their cultures, and their value system, and due to this, our cultures can create a better tomorrow. Thus, if we want to bring out a change in this world, it should be our underlying cultures that should be looked into, for they have all the solutions to our ideas and dreams.

My Ramadan Memories

It's a festive season once again

That time of the year has come again, when the faithful fast for a month and host sumptuous Iftars and Suhours, and when many flock together and gather as one family during Ramadan. For me, a non-Muslim, Ramadan in the UAE holds a different yet significant meaning. Ramadan always has fond memories for me.

I clearly remember my years in primary and middle school, when Ramadan used to fall in the month of September. School used be for three hours from 8.00–11.00 a.m., and all of us happily enjoyed the very short working hours and running home to enjoy those extra free hours outside school. I remember those Ramadan quizzes, which always ended in a lucky draw (that never was lucky for me).

Then as the years rolled by, Ramadan was in August and then in July. I remember the times when I spent the holiday month of Ramadan in Dubai. I had a sneak peak and delved into Ramadan and Eid festivities, or I had a late-night dinner after Iftar hours. I fondly remember the afternoons and evenings I spent acquainting myself with the Ramadan culture.

With the passing of time, I also grew in tolerance and knowledge of this season, and I give my due respects and wishes to all those who observe it sincerely and with devotion. I simply love the way the UAE celebrates this, making it holy and revered for the faithful, as well as a special occasion for everyone. I cannot forget the generosity of the mosques and organisations who create the big camps, where anyone can come to break their fast. The Ramadan care packages of which I was a part made me learn the importance of this month as a season of giving.

Ramadan is indeed a time when I bond and enjoy with my family and friends. I also remind myself of the values of religious tolerance and coexistence.

Patriotism

Your country is your future

When one's country celebrates its national day, and when the nation's flag is put up, a true patriot's mind sings the national anthem. On such an occasion, don't you feel that patriotism is the greatest gift to your country? Patriotism simply means love for or devotion to one's country. All letters spell out what patriotism is: P is for people; A is for allegiance; T is for truth; R is for respect; I is for innovation; O is for oath; T is for tolerance; I is for indivisible; S is for sacrifice; and M is for mother.

We the people are a part of the future of our country – where it will stand in the world, the path it will take, and how the nations of the world recognize its uniqueness. Wherever we are born and whichever nationality we belong to, it is our duty to swear allegiance to our country, to serve it in times of peace and war and with all our minds and souls. Every nation is born through times that have shown the truth of life, the pains and struggles one has to go through. As citizens and residents of our country, we have to respect it with all our hearts. We students, as future global citizens, can bring about great innovations in our country so that the journey of its progress is very remarkable and unforgettable. We must take an oath that we will preserve the name and honour of our country and also imply the sense of brotherhood within us. This sense of brotherhood can be invoked in us by living with tolerance, which can stop all wars and bloodshed with one hand. The proverb, "United we stand; divided we fall," reminds me that all of us should remain indivisible in our loyalty to our country; we should stand by it during times of tribulations. Sacrifice is what we should be ready to face in order to keep up the glory of our nation. Last, our country is our mother who has nurtured us, and who deserves a lot of love and gratitude from us.

Patriotism may not be so loud that everyone around notices it. It need not be just waving the flag or singing the national anthem. But it is the best gift, though silence, that shows how deeply you regard your country, your motherland.

Human Trafficking

The sad situation of many

The Immoral Trafficking Prevention Act (ITPA) of India, the fundamental rights mentioned in the big political bible of the Indian Constitution, legally prohibhit what everybody calls human trafficking. But do you think there has been a full stop to that crime with the above mentioned measures? I don't think so.

People are frequently illegally trafficked through India for the purposes of commercial sexual exploitation and forced or bonded labour. Women and girls are trafficked within the country for the purposes of commercial sexual exploitation and forced marriage, especially in those areas where the sex ratio is highly skewed in favour of men. A significant portion of children are subjected to forced labour as factory workers, domestic servants, beggars, and agriculture workers, and they have been used as armed combatants by some terrorist and insurgent groups. I feel this is totally wrong and immoral. It has been sixty-eightn years since our country became independent and democratic, and it is so shameful to say a large number of the population is being exploited for wrong purposes. Children dream of a school life, but they are kidnapped and locked up in the confines of a factory or a terrorist camp. Women dream of an educated life where they can earn a living with dignity, but they are kidnapped and sold for awful purposes. Isn't that sad?

But it isn't enough that the better, luckier sect of the country thinks and raises this issue in front of the elected parliament. The government should also think about the underprivileged, especially when trafficking goes hand in hand with corruption. We citizens need to pressure the leaders. Let's hope that the Modi-Sarkar can do something about this.

Destroying the Spirit of Freedom

Restrictions for everything kills the spirit of the country

Some headlines of March 2015 are questioning the democratic ideals of India. One is the ban of the trade and possession of beef in Maharashtra, which I consider crazy. The constitution says that India is a secular country that equally recognises all religions. Yet the "Hindu spirit" driven politicians of the Maharashtra government do not seem to abide by the rules of the country when they say that Hindu's can't eat beef, and so the whole state shouldn't eat it.

This is a cosmopolitan state, and the needs of diverse communities need to be tolerated beyond the printed slogan of "Unity in Diversity". Even though the ruling party supports Hinduism at large, they simply have no right to make this move, which also closes the trade of beef, a profession of many that are the only breadwinners of their families. The High Court shouldn't have allowed such a play with religious sentiments. Such laws are the stepping stones to communal riots. Instead of closing abattoirs, the government should place a check on and eradicate rising epidemics like the swine flu. In a huge country with multiple issues, the concerns of a large public, of the poor and needy, should be more important than those regarding a particular sect of society.

The latest addition that depicted the narrow-mindedness of the government is the ban of the BBC documentary *India's Daughter*. The man who raped a physiotherapy intern is indeed arrogant and shameless to put the blame of the crime on the victim by saying, "She should have dressed modestly and shouldn't have fought back, but allowed the rape to go on." These remarks shouldn't have prompted the censor board to ask BBC to pull the video. The girl's father rightly said that the video would have given the people an insight to the dirty attitude of rapists. Only the truth behind the curtains can bring to light what is often ignored. Banning such videos will only increase the number of illegal downloads. Let's wait and see whether the narrow-minded board can reverse its decision.

Rights for Female Children

Human rights

In many places in the world, girls are not treated equally with boys. Girls have to face many challenges in society, including violence and discrimination. The UN took an important step to put an end to such injustices when it declared 11 October as the International Day of the Girl Child. This day focuses on the challenges faced by girls and highlights their rights.

The newspapers have a lot to report on the safety of young girls, particularly challenges and threats of rape and abuse. In many primitive areas, a young girl is considered a curse. A girl child is made to listen to remarks of contempt: "A girl? Why not a son?" When she enters the world, even before she can see and identify the world around her, she is often killed or abandoned.

Every girl has the right to live and grow up to be someone who is meant to be successful. I am a girl, and I feel so lucky that I have no obstacles like this to face in life. There is still a tremendous amount of work to be done to ensure that all girls receive the same opportunity in education and that each girl is empowered to believe that she is part of the next generation of change makers.

A single Malala Yousafzai is not enough to get rights for all girls, especially the right of education for girls. Every lucky girl on this planet needs to bring out our inner Yousafzai that is hiding within us. We need to help out the less fortunate girls who are either married as children or made to face trafficking.

Eliminating Violence against Women

Doesn't a woman have rights to ahimsa?

Violence against women is a violation of their rights, and it is a consequence of discrimination in law, in practice, and in the persisting inequalities between men and women. Violence against women and girls is not inevitable. If we all join hands, it can be brought under control. Violence against women continues to be a global pandemic. To recognise the need for a non-violent world, the United Nations has declared November 25 as International Day for the Elimination of Violence against Women.

I, as a young woman, am really concerned even though I have been brought up under safe circumstances. In this world, any girl or woman can face violence at any time. Humans are racing against time to invent and develop, but they do not find time to do the least for the mothers, daughters, and sisters of the world to help them live in a non-violent world. It is not really possible to have a violence-free world. However, it is imperative that both sexes work towards this goal of protecting the makers of the next generation. November 25 is used as a time to speak out on this issue, but I think that it's time to let every day be a day to speak out for the elimination of violence against women.

2014 Nobel Peace Prize

Making the world better

It was indeed wonderful to read that a girl who fought for education for all girls, and a man who is from my country, won the Nobel Peace Prize this year.

As activists for children's rights, Malala Yousafzai and Kailash Satyarthi, are deserving winners of this coveted prize. The winners symbolise the importance of relations between India and Pakistan. Awarding them shows how people from both countries have stood up for the common cause of educational rights. Yousafzai has proved herself to be an icon for education for girls ever since she was shot by the Taliban. She has faced the situation boldly and expressed her demands and views on the issue, which is an ongoing one in Asia. She has shown that even when facing great challenges, one can be a hero when fighting for people's cause.

Satyarthi has showed great personal courage in staging various forms of protests and demonstrations (all peaceful), and in focusing on the grave exploitation of children for financial gain. He has also contributed to the development of important international conventions on children's rights. The world would be a much better place if it had more people like them.

A Disagreement

Conflicts and battles – can they move the society for the better?

Ought a disagreement always bear a negative result? Is it always a barrier to progress? Does it have to break down mutual understanding, unity, and cooperation? Does it really induce differences? These are what many attribute to disagreements arising between two individuals, groups of people or communities, and even organizations or various countries. But such narrow-minded people are blind to the genesis of ideas, innovations, and wonders to which a disagreement can lead. In fact, the father of our nation has said, "Honest disagreement is often a good sign of progress."

You might wonder whether the everyday disagreements between children (especially teenagers) and their parents can actually bring about progress. If that disagreement or difference in opinion is valid and candid, then it brings changes for the good. My parents and I have disagreed upon many things, such as my choice of activities or my approach towards various issues and problems. This has helped me to open my mind and change from a single perspective to a multi-dimensional one, thus helping me to think from all angles before reaching a conclusion or decision.

When someone disagrees with your viewpoint, you might sometimes feel you are wrong and he is right. Then that little voice urges you to step into that person's shoes and ponder about what he said. That may change you or your thought process for the better. You may also have a mental conflict, or what one might call confusion, in choosing between two choices. The disagreements between various thoughts in your head are the challenges that can make you a mature thinker.

Can debates and disagreement ever cause destruction? My answer is yes and no. Sometimes people disagree with their rulers and take to outdoor protests, which can cause unpleasant scenes of police or army controlling the hysteric population, leading to clashes and stampedes. But what about political debates in a parliament session? The Lok Sabha and State Assembly sessions are full of them. These arguments are instrumental in the passing of new bills and making of new laws. If there was no disagreement, India wouldn't have had a constitution. Without opinions shared on the table, how can the government come to know the plausible responses of the people? Democracies, and even free-minded monarchies like Denmark, function best through the system of parley and discourse in their decision making procedures. Debates, especially those we see on news channels on prevailing issues, help lawmakers come to know what everybody feels and thus come up with the best solution. Therefore aren't dialogues and disagreements of great help here?

A disagreement within the scientific community can lead to scientists thinking of and coming up with revolutionary ideas and. The periodic table and the structure of an atom have been discovered due to the fact that scientists disagreed with the existing model. Even in stories and movies, if there are no cases of conflict between the protagonist and antagonist, or between the central characters who are on an adventure, the plot can't progress and the fun and interest is gone.

A disagreement – big or small, important or trivial – can actually be for the better and not just have a dark side. In the words of the social philosopher Eric Hoffer, "The beginning of thought is in disagreement – not only with others but also with ourselves."

Best Fictional Character:
Sherlock Holmes

Indulging in fiction

October 2014 signifies 125 years of Sir Arthur Conan Doyle's Sherlock Holmes. This character has fascinated me since I was in primary school. I read the "Hound of the Baskervilles" when I was first introduced to crime and detective fiction, and I was hooked. The way the story unfolds, the sequence of events, and the methods of investigation and deduction executed by Holmes continue to amaze me even now.

The plot and the presentation of clues are often like a puzzle that makes us think of many possible solutions – but never the right one. The stories are filled with thrills and action that surpasses many of today's detective fictions and movies.

Reading a Sherlock Holmes novel is often like watching a movie. We don't feel like leaving the story halfwaydone. As I read, the story is imprinted in my mind, and I am able to visualise it. I find myself taking on the character of Dr Watson, who follows Holmes during investigations and always admires him, yet he is never able to crack the mysteries himself.

Sir Arthur Conan Doyle's intelligence is solely responsible for the wonders of Sherlock Holmes, and if you ask me, Sherlock Holmes is indeed the best fictional character of all ages. How I wish he was real!

Does the Information Age Mean That We Are Losing Important Historical Information?

In the tehnology age of the twenty-first century

As the years pass by, people tend to be more curious about unearthing the hidden secrets of this magical world. Also, the technology has improved, keeping up with the demands of the growing population and the changing lifestyles. We can neither agree nor disagree with the statement, "The information age means that we are losing important historical information." The information age – or the technology age, as it is commonly referred to – has both positive and negative impacts on the world of history, the common past.

Advancement in technology helps people research better on our history (or on anything). People who love to research our past – archaeologists, historians, geologists, palaeontologists, and many more – depend on technology for effective results. Digital innovations have gifted us new equipment like X-rays and laser scanners to detect clues hidden beneath the earth's visible surface. Global positioning systems (GPS) have been useful in various explorations. Technology, through its vast array of dictionaries and decoders, has given us a helping hand and made it easier to decipher different codes, signs, and ancient languages. Google and Wikipedia can help students with their projects with great ease. Thus technology can give us the historical information we need, making life for students a cup of tea.

However, the extensive use of technology might have curbed the interest and insight with which people learnt history. Many historians and archaeologists learn more about the past by experimenting and trying to solve the unsolved jigsaw puzzles. But most of the people (including history students) are now the victims of technology, which makes it easier to acquire information. This has reduced the original purpose of historical information – to discover and learn. Technology is also imperfect at times. All the information we get from the Internet is not be correct. When a new piece of information is excavated, different versions of it are posted, and it is difficult to identify the truth.

As time flies, authentic historical information is slipping from our hands. Technology is all about making mistakes and discovering something new out of these, whereas history teaches us not to make mistakes. Information technology has led to a lack of interest in what has remained in the past, with ever growing interest in the future. This adversely affects the main motive of history: to love the past. When the world around us changes, we tend to forget what was there before us and before these machines. We might be losing important losing important historical information due to the information age.

In the current scenario, the historical information mankind currently possesses faces serious threats from the advancing new media age. If we humans know how to manage our resources and technology, and if we understand the individual and unique importance of the past, present, and future, then the information age will not wipe out the important information of our past.

Books vs. Movies

In today's technical world

Once, I asked my friend, "Did you like *The Christmas Carol*?" I expected a comment on the book.

My friend's answer amazed me. "Oh, yes! I liked the snowy scenery and the three ghosts, and Tiny Tim looked very cute." With more film adaptations of famous books, the golden age of reading is on the decline.

Today's generation loves watching movies, but I feel that there is no real entertainment other than reading books. Books open the doors to a new world of imagination. Books help us to widen our mental horizons and give us creative and innovative approaches to life. Many people love watching films based on popular books, and some are eternal favourites. Whereas films can give us only temporary happiness, books give us eternal joy. The youth love watching movies based on books because they can watch their favourite heroes on screen, admire visual effects, and enjoy the music. This attitude has given reading a back seat in their lives.

I do not mean to say that movies are worse than the books on which they are based. Some movies are classics that have portrayed the story with excellence, and their respective books became more popular due to the movies. One such example is *Gone with the Wind*, based on Margaret Mitchell's classic.

But watching movies do not always help us to perceive the message of the story. When we are lost in the artificial movie world, we often overlook the real theme of the story. However, books give us a clear idea about what the story is. Reading also helps us improve our vocabulary with different kinds of words, phrases, and idioms. Movies may show the story's setting, but only through books will we get a complete knowledge about various characters and their attitudes, places, and lifestyles. We may not be able to watch movies wherever we go, but books have held out their arms to us, waiting to be loved.

Don't you think that books are better than movies?

Freedom of Press

The media that keeps us informed and updated

We all know that freedom of speech and expression is one of our basic rights, and freedom of the press is especially important to protect these rights. In fact, it is the freedom of the press, from print media to televsion news, that helps the globe to move forward. World Press Freedom Day is celebrated on May 3 every year. This day has been recognised to reaffirm the fundamental principles that ensure freedom of the press globally, to defend the media from attacks on their independence, and to pay tribute to those journalists who have lost their lives.

The media has been an integral forum for those who have needed a platform to speak their minds, and for those whose problems never have been recognised. Though the media may have abused its freedom at times to get ahead of each other in delivering news first, it has always served mankind since time immemorial. I salute all those journalists, especially the ones who have been through tough times, for sacrificing a lot of comforts, time, and even their safety, for all our awareness and for those people who need a voice. If there was no press, many of us wouldn't be able to speak our thoughts out loud. Press freedom is something to always be cherished.

Television Is Universal

Life without television?

In light of World Television Day on November 21, one should note the use of television is ever increasing, and it has diversified from simply being a tool for watching movies and programmes. The television has changed our lives in so many ways, and I think it is amazing. It entertains us, teaches us, broadens our horizons, and has broken geographical, linguistic, and cultural barriers. Television brings us news every day from every corner of the world instantly, and it focuses attention on major issues facing the world. It produces results and has been a symbol of communication. It also gives us the comfort of watching movies from home without having to purchase tickets.

Television has evolved. It has gaming capacities with different providers. Internet television is yet another option, with YouTube on a big screen, and now video conferencing is done on televisions as well. Earlier these activities were a status symbol, but now they are practically a necessity. No wonder the United Nations has a day to honour television!

Future of Bullying

Does technology make unsecure and unsafe lives?

In the context of the recent cybercrime cases, as stated in the newspaper report "Stop Cyber-crime Army to be Set up in Kerala Schools", published on June 23, 2015, I feel that this a crime that cannot be completely eradicated by simply teaching people not to communicate with strangers and give away personal details. Rather, people who are interested in bullying, teasing, and torturing others via the Internet are the ones who have to be taught not to lure innocent users into revealing personal information. With respect to the country of India, crimes in cyberspace is a challenge awaiting the government's attention. In today's world and in many aspects, criminals have the upper hand, and in most cases they manage to escape punishment. The one who is left to suffer is the ignorant victim of this new generation of crime.

I am not surprised to hear that children of the new generation have admitted to creating a negative online experience for their fellow students during their school years. All this is not just due to exposure to wrong movies, websites, surroundings, company, and friendships. Parents are also to be blamed when their children head down a wrong path. This is now an issue that is getting out of the hands of families and neighbourhoods. If the government cooperates with civilians, they can work together towards the prevention of cybercrime. If we do that, the Internet may be less threatening in the future.

Live Your Life – But Not on Social Media

Social media should be

stopped with a computer

Social media is something that has helped us reach out to anyone and everyone with one click. Be it friendship, marketing, awareness campaigns, or popularity, social media has given them all a presence that wasn't possible more than a decade ago.

Philosophers might say social media can have degrading effects on our lives by distracting us from our work, but today, life seems to be empty without having a Facebook account, or tweeting, or using Instagram from time to time – isn't it? I firmly believe that life can be lived outside social media, and there is a lot to be discovered and experienced! You can count on me for this, because I am not there on social media.

Social media can be a benefit or a nuisance, depending on how we use it. But it has now become an indispensable part of our lives, and we should thank those who have created this marvel of communication.

Let's not forget that hashtags, tweets, and the like are not what life is about, and they will not change your life. I am not a user, and I don't think my existence is dull without this; rather, I need not be troubled by the perils of hashtags, likes, and tweets. These are simply media, and it is you who is supposed to live the life you want to live and do the work for which you want to be recognized.

The Cell Phone Revolution

A real time helper or a nuisance?

Every morning, many people wake up by hearing a melody of alarm from their mobile phones. At school, one can hear the excited voices of students: "I got an iPhone 6!" "Hey, have you heard how amazing the Samsung Galaxy S5 is?" You can always find Beats covering someone's ear, but again, they're connected to a cell phone.

I do agree that an expensive cell phone gives one some extra glitter in society. But what impact does it have on the real you? You may change in a good way – or a bad way. You might be up-to-date with the events around the globe thanks to Wi-Fi and 4G connections twenty-four seven. You may fashion your vocabulary with LOL, OMG, TTYL, BRB, and more. Who knows – you might be a Guinness record holder for the most phone calls per day. And of course, your Facebook status is updated every hour. Photography now easily fits in your pocket. Songs and movies are always handy – how cool!

That's a jolly way of life. But, dear friends, don't forget that life is also made for serious work. Cell phones may be a boon, but working on it the whole day can make it a bane. Cell phones not only distract you from work, but they also cause a lot of health hazards – eye diseases, cancer of various kinds, and migraines are caused due to harmful radiation. Attending to phone calls the whole day actually steals your mind, if you don't realise it. But many people don't seem to bother. The "Let the philosopher tell, but science will protect us" attitude has created revolutions all over the world. If you think about it, cell phones are not daily necessities for a school child, but a luxury.

I scratch my head and remind myself that excessive mobile usage can transform the formal English language to an informal one, using "dis" and "dat", to the point that sometimes teachers stare sadly at some of our essays.

I am not totally against cell phones, but this cell phone revolution should not decide one's future.

Harsh Eid Climate

Unbearable climate is not a restraint for celebration

The climate was harsh for Eid. It was too sunny and for many the heat was almost unbearable during the month of Ramadan as well. Yet, when it comes to the purpose of fasting, the Muslims perform their duties without hesitation despite the challenges of summer. Thus, Eid would obviously be a respite for them.

But Eid is also a time for everybody in this country to be together with their families and enjoy the festivities around the country. Thanks to the colourful celebration put up by the authorities in the UAE, not many would actually find the Eid holidays boring.

We are fortunate in this country, where a diverse global community live together. Every year, Eid is not just the end of fast for Muslims, but also a time for everybody to relish the fun, joy and spirit of the occasion.

Anticipating School

New class, fresh faces, a new year embraces

As the end of the two-month summer break is approaching, many of us pupils view the end of holidays from different perspectives.

For many pupils who follow the Indian curriculum, summer holidays come right during the academic year, which has already begun in April. So, these two months are not just relaxation and rejuvenation, but a time to complete our assignments and projects, and to prepare for the upcoming exams.

For many others, the end of this vacation is synonymous with a new academic year. Pupils are buying new books, new stationery, and new uniforms. All will be filled with the excitement of greeting a new school year and perhaps even a new set of friends.

However, thanks to the advent of technology, the fearsome burden of heavy books, exams, and projects makes schools a foreseeable nightmare. It results in remarks from pupils, asking, "Who wants to go to school?"

But trust me: the beginning of school can be wonderful and full of surprises hidden for us in the months to come. That's why I'm really excited for school to reopen.

Spreading Literacy

A learned world is a distant dream

Can we imagine what life would be like if we didn't know how to read and write? I read recently there are more than 774 million adults around the world who do not know how to read and write. This is a very sad fact. Everyone knows that a basic education that gives one at least reading and writing skills is the right of every individual, and it's an important tool for progress and social development. Let us be reminded what it means to receive a basic education. The UN and UNESCO recognize 8 September every year as World Literacy Day, to honour every human's right to education.

The world would be totally different if every child was able to go to school. World leaders should not concentrate primarily on strengthening international political ties, increasing nuclear deals, or improving trade relations. Instead, they must ensure that their most important resources, their people, are given education in order to secure nations' future.

Let's remind ourselves of the importance of education and lend a helping hand to those who dream of literacy.

My Dubai, My Expo

Getting a global identity

As flags of the upcoming Expo 2020 decorate Dubai, I am sure that Dubai is the unparalleled candidate whose innovations are excellent beyond measures. Dubai is the land of progress, wonder, dreams, and reality. You name it, and Dubai has it. The high level of infrastructure and technology makes it at par with the big names on the face of the Earth, such as the United States and the European Union. The UAE economy attracts many migrants to dig out their pots of gold.

Every individual needs safety and security in his or her life, and it is what makes up one of the gold stars of this city. As a teenage girl, I have no fear of walking the streets, even at night. When we are asleep, there are people awake to take care of us at the darkest hour. Dubai also does not like to see anyone sad, jobless, or disappointed.

Dubai is a magical land of opportunities for every field – education, health, business, aviation, and more. In the fifteen years of my life spent here, I have never felt left out or cornered, bored or listless, depressed or unhappy. The marvellous Dubai has lots in store for me – clubs, sports, adventure, fun activities, and more. Dubai has always answered the anticipation, needs, and wants of my family and everyone here.

I am deeply grateful to H. H. Sheikh Mohammed bin Rashid Al Maktoum and his predecessors for transforming the sandy desert to a magical land full of life and development. The vision of such leaders has resulted in the current status of Dubai and everybody out of here.

As I think of Dubai hosting the Expo 2020, I will be doing my final year of undergraduation in geosciences. I cannot wait for the time when I, as a twenty-two-year-old, will see Dubai showcasing itself to the entire globe.

Dubai – Truly Capable

Now what about an Olympics?

Upon hearing news about the possibility of Dubai placing an Olympic bid, I wasn't surprised. Dubai is a very obvious candidate and has potential to be an excellent host to the world's largest sporting extravaganza.

I feel the success of Dubai's bid to host the Expo 2020 should be carried forward to other events as well. The multinational and multicultural city is a place that has wonders, keeping the world astonished. Dubai is such a global centre, where the world can come together to celebrate, play, and achieve. It's not enough that the host city has more than sufficient sporting arenas or an amazing sport history. It should be Olympic in community and spirit, which the magical land of Dubai has always shown.

If Dubai is placing a bid to host the Olympics, I would be happy to say that the UAE would indeed be an awesome host!

Progress Is Not an Illusion

Moving ahead

Progress can hold different descriptions for different people. As George Orwell said, "Progress is not an illusion; it happens, but is slow and invariably dissapointing." It is not just about moving ahead; it's about getting better and then moving forward with your plan.

Most of the time we find ourselves stuck at one point even if we have spent a lot of time on it. I have faced it several times, especially when I was trying to learn different tunes on my keyboard. It is part and parcel with progress, but it is not an obstacle. If a procrastinator considers progress to always be slow, he is wrong. Progress comes about only when we put our hearts and minds into it, without paying much attention to the time going into it.

For instance, history tells us about the progress of politics and governance in various nations. The establishment of equal opportunities for men and women is a good example. For certain countries, it has happened right after independence, as in the case of India. For other countries, it took years of struggle, like in the UK and the United States. Progress need not be as quick as one may expect, but it definitely happens if one has a great interest, desire, and will for it to happen. Progress doesn't come easily, but you are in control of your own progress, and a nation is in control of its own progress, which makes it easier to approach.

Progress is something meant for empowerment and satisfaction. It is something that comes to those who chase it. But the time it takes to answer your call may not be definite. Progress can be slow and disappointing or fast and encouraging; it is a matter of destiny. Nevertheless, we must continue to persevere till we have seen the ultimate peak of progress.

Is Hapiness a Measure of Progress?

What is true progress?

Scene 1: A meeting at an advertising firm

Boss: The company had been behind its targets for the past five months. I've seen that most of you are distracted and insincere at work.

HRM: Sir, most of us are unhappy. We work for extended hours and get limited holidays, yet we don't get the right pay. How can there be productivity?

Boss: I don't care. Come what may, however much you grumble, I need profit. You give up happy times when you work here; otherwise, just resign.

An employee: But, sir, how can we move ahead without worker contentment?

Scene 2: A high school classroom discussion

Girl 1: I work very hard, and yet my grades are dropping. This is so depressing.

Girl 2: Life is so stressful and disturbing. I simply can't focus.

Boy 3: Gone are the days when I was always happy. Gone is my outstanding performance. My negative aura is bringing me down.

And this is not all.

What makes different people happy? Is it love, peace, contentment, success, or wealth? Don't you think the idea of joy differs for everybody? And what about progress? Now progress, just like happiness, can take different aspects altogether. In today's world, progress can be financial, professional, academic, and even emotional. But do we actually want this in life? Are we happy about working towards the achievement of goals of the types I mentioned earlier?

Whitney Houston had everything any lady would have wanted – name, fame, wealth, and a lovely daughter. But she was a victim of substance abuse. Why? It's simply because she was depressed, and that prevented her from progressing spiritually. Remember, the world might be yours. But if your mind and soul fails to find joy, peace, and contentment, you can't progress smoothly in life, even if you toil round the clock.

Let's analyse two nations. The United States boasts one of the highest GDPs in the world and the lowest percentage of poverty. But is everyone there happy? Is nobody mumbling about the state of affairs or regretting life at work and home? Even the very influential Steve Jobs wasn't always happy. This lack of happiness is preventing the powerful United States from achieving the best and progressing towards the greatest heights. They might be progressing in technology, communications, and weapons, but the true essence of holistic progress, which includes personal and spiritual progress, is missing there.

Take the case of Costa Rica. It is not wealthy; it is not the land of billionaires. But Costa Rica is one of the richest countries on earth. Why? In a Tico's words, "Nowhere else can you live as well, as long, or as happily … or as easily as here in Costa Rica. We have grown, in a unique way from rags to riches, because no one sheds a tear."

Happiness is a mental or emotional state of well-being defined by positive emotions like contentment. But it is not only that. I feel that happiness is a fuel that propels a person to move ahead towards his goals. The happier the person, the greater will be his focus on the task at hand, and the greater will be his progress in that work. If you were to measure the science of happiness and link it to productivity in a particular industry, it's likely happiness of the staff is responsible for that.

Time and again, many luminaries have proved that nobody has been successful with a pensive state of mind. As a disturbed and angry student, Albert Einstein couldn't perform well. But as a scientist, he was happy, and that lead him to be the greatest. What about Sherlock Holmes? If he wasn't happy as a detective, if he didn't enjoy solving mysteries, and if he wasn't optimistic, would he have progressed and answered the most complicated of mysteries?

Don't you think this issue also matters in society? Many of us perceive social progress as the idea that societies improve in terms of their social, political, and economic structures. But remember, the genesis of society begins with an individual, and in order for every society to grow and develop, positivity and well-being for all is crucial. The success of each individual can impact the community, however small or large it may be. Unless humanity smiles and there is joy all around, no such impact can be made to take civilization forward.

Do you get a taste of joy and yet feel miserable? Take a moment to reflect: "Am I really enjoying the lasting happiness that I've always wanted?" Progress indeed leads to happiness, which is life in itself. If you are moving forward in your life and are progressing personally, professionally, and emotionally, then you will be happy. It's only on stagnation that we will wilt like flowers. And mind you, happiness is just not about joy and laughter. For those who are victims of violence and war, happiness means peace and silence.

Pablo Neruda said in his poem "Keeping Quiet",
> If we were not so single-minded
> about keeping our lives moving,
> and for once could do nothing,
> perhaps a huge silence
> might interrupt this sadness
> of never understanding ourselves
> and of threatening ourselves with death.

This is what progress should be all about: caring for others and not being self-centred.

Politician parlours, the mansions of millionaires, the offices of business honchos, the cramped quarters of labourers – for any cohort of society, in order to achieve personal and social progress, there should be an element of felicity that can be realized from within. It is happiness that leads to growth, development, progress, and prosperity.

India's Space Venture

Making a mark out of earth

It was 6.30 a.m., and I was getting ready to go to school when an Indian news channel proudly declared the successful launch of the Mangalyaan.

The entry of India's Mars Orbiter Mission (MOM) is indeed of great importance for the country and its space history. It is cost effective, and it had already gathered praise and compliments from renowned scientists and space organisations.

What's more amazing is that only the United States, Europe, and Russia have previously sent missions to Mars. India is the first country to succeed on its first attempt. This achievement improves India's global position in space technology. India's success substantiates the fact that it is always developing in various areas of scientific research, which will certainly inspire the younger generation of the country.

I am very proud of my country's success, and I hope that one day I can contribute to the space history of India.

World Post Day

Messaging

On October 9, more than 150 countries recognise postal workers and postal services by celebrating World Post Day. The days may be over when the postman knocks at the door and shouts, "You've got a letter!" However, postal services – or the so-called snail mail services – are still in operation. Sending letters around the world to reach the nearest post office, if not your doorstep, is still fairly common.

Even in the era of email and text messages, the postman cannot be forgotten. Letters still remain a persuasive and very personal way of communicating. Postal services have also played an important role in the history and development of countries, from the times of pigeon post.

The presence of post offices is still recognised by the issuing and purchasing of stamps to add to collectors' albums. The wiring of telegrams by some countries, and sending letters instead of emails in order to better display emotions, are competitive advantages that keep postal technology alive. I don't think post offices can be replaced by technology.

International Day of Yoga

All for a healthy lifestyle

June 21, 2015: Indeed a day to remember and be proud of my Indian culture, as the UN has declared the twenty-first day of June to be the International Day of Yoga. More than 175 countries around the world have observed it, celebrating the reason and the essence of the existence of the more than 8 million asanas for a healthy body, mind, and soul. The UAE too was at the forefront when it came to celebrating this day. The Indian Consulate took this opportunity to organise a large scale event, which resulted in the event at Al Wasl Football ground in Al Jadaf, Dubai. People from various walks of life have been filling the spaces with their mats since, I guess, 6 p.m. The excitement was building up in each one of us. At 8 p.m., the programme began with a video message from the Hon'ble Prime Minister of India Shri Narendra Modi. The Consul General of India, HE Anurag Bhushan flagged off the event in the presence of many dignitaries like five-time World Amateur Boxing champion and Indian Olympic medallist M.C. Mary Kom and Major-General Nasser Al Sayed Abdualrazak Al Razooqi, the president of the UAE Karate and Taekwondo Federation and member of the UAE National Olympic Committee as chief guests, as well as many yoga gurus from various corners of India and the United States. It was a refreshing session with teachings about yoga, besides doing the asanas. The postures we took – the exercises we did – weren't very difficult. That one hour was very refreshing. It provided me a moment of peace, calmness, and inner joy.

The event was a great one, and indeed memorable for every Indian who takes pride in their centuries old culture and traditions.

Breast Cancer Awareness Month

Be aware and healthy

As October is over, we can look back and reflect on a lot of pink memories throughout the breast cancer awareness month. Breast cancer awareness has been a campaign that has been strongly supported by the authorities and the public alike. Many organisations and individuals have taken up this cause and spread awareness in various ways.

The Safe and Sound campaign has always attracted huge crowds to its pink book sale and the Pink Walkathon. The opportunity to raise funds and enjoy entertainment attracts huge crowds in solidarity for this cause.

Even at my school, students were encouraged to wear pink ribbons on their uniforms for the entire month. The message was spread through the school's Twitter handle. The student's council came up with the idea of wearing pink hairbands and shailas (head scarves) to support the cause wholeheartedly.

Several organisations have spread the word in different ways. Awareness and early detection are key factors in saving lives from breast cancer. It is quite nice to know that a previously unknown cause is now taken seriously by many. Let this kind of public awareness in healthcare continue to make this place a healthier place to live.

Looking Back at a Year of Fear – 2014

Times have changed – often for the worse

As I look back on this year, there are many great moments and achievements that are worthy of cherishing. Dubai's record-breaking fireworks display on January 1, the appointment of Narendra Modi as the prime minister of India, Germany's victory of the FIFA World Cup, the success story of Mangalyaan, the successful landing of Rosetta spacecraft's Philae probe on Comet 67P, the opening of Dubai Tram, and the launching of Plan 2021 are some of them.

However, overpowering their goodness are those terrible moments that have cost a great deal to many. The recent attack on the military school in Peshawar is just one of them; many innocent children became martyrs through no fault of theirs. Terror attacks around the world and political uprisings have created a global turmoil. The violence surrounding the Sochi Olympics undermined Russia's security. The mysterious disappearance and crash of two flights from Malaysian Airlines is yet another tragic instance. The growing tensions between Israel and Hamas have claimed many lives, and Gaza has become a land strip of violence and sorrow. Daesh came out with events that left everybody in shock, such as the beheading of civilians, radical movements, and all sorts of terror activities that rocked the world.

The rate of rape that women face has increased rapidly, and the security of women in the world is unsure. Many people have had to face a gruesome death when they did not expect it, like the American schoolteacher who was recently stabbed in an Abu Dhabi mall. Random bombings in many parts of the world by various terrorist groups have filled the pages of various newspapers on a daily basis. Ebola has rocked nations and has wiped out millions, but that I must say that was not really a human error. There is an endless list of such disasters, so let's wait and see whether 2015 will be a better year.

My

Poems

Memories

As I walked
Down the leafy road,
The golden scenery
Struck me
With thoughts so numerous
And memories so old.

I remembered my babyhood,
When I was a carefree baby:
My dad playing with me;
My mother singing a sweet
lullaby.
When my first day at school
flashed,
When I cried in my class
And I got a yummy chocolate,
And when I played with pals
on grass
As I grew older,
Homework became usual,
With lots of work to do,
With time so casual.
And then I come to now,
With the world changing around me.
I stare at time and say, "Wow!"
As I go further
Down the leafy road
With thoughts so endless.
I remember
Time flies,
But memories don't.

A Holiday to Remember

When I shut my eyes
And lie on the bed,
With the stars above my head,
I remember my holiday
That just went away.

I remember the yawn
That came with the dawn.
I remember the jog
Near the lake, through the misty fog.
I remember my breakfast of cake,
And my table near the lake.
I remember the news I read
Of some happenings that I dread.
I remember playing hide and seek
When I hid behind that huge teak.
I remember that delicious lunch:
"Mmm ... Munch, munch, munch!"
I remember that chat,
When I was disturbed by a cat and a rat.
I remember playing football,
Crashing a window and hearing an angry call.
I remember the fascinating book I read,
Which will always stay in my head.
I think of all this
And wish such a holiday
Will come on another day.

The Pink Ribbon

As I looked upon the calendar,
A small ribbon stuck me.
So pinky, so girly,
But it had a great message to speak.

"Breast Cancer Awareness," it said.
Pink ribbons all around –
A great message to spread.
For all our mothers,
For their precious health,
For their lives.

The earth needs moms –
Moms with health.
Breast cancer is a demon
Devouring our desires.

So let's join hands
In this cause of love,
Against the demon of breast cancer.

O pink ribbon, I salute you
For the marvellous work you do:
For protecting our mothers,
For protecting our love.

So is Life

Flying high up in the sky
Is a swallow so white,
With its orange beak
And tails forked so wide.
It flies on and on,
Across seas and oceans,
Across mountains and hills,
Across plateaus and plains.
But one day it will come down
To build a nest
And welcome babies.
Tending to them till they grow
With wings and tails so forked.

Dreams get high
Floating in space,
But one day we'll realise
Ups and downs never stay away.
So is fun and duty;
So is enjoyment and suffering;
So is success and hardwork;
So is life!

Packing – Confusing but Amusing

What a hustleand bustle is life!
At home, school, work
But holiday time,
A free spot time,
Is made by packing –
A commotion worse than ever.

Life is full of humour and problems,
And so is packing.
Stuffing into suitcases,
Things crumpled and stiff,
And crossing of the checklist

But at night, we remember
The misery of life.
With no comb, no toothbrush,
No cream, no soap.

"Who told you to pack that now?"
"Why did you say so then?"
Certain language not good for me
Adds to the background music.

And finally midsummer night's dream is fulfilled:
Packing finishes in hustle and bustle
Amidst all confusion,
But for one goal, one motive –
A happy holiday time!

Nature and Man – A Huge Contrast

The sun shining brightly,
The birds singing sweetly,
The breeze blowing swiftly.
Plants and animals waking up
and living to the new glory of the day.
Nature's experiencing and spreading joy daily.

Polluting the environment,
Terrorising the land daily,
Fighting and hating forever,
Killing the happy creatures around,
Destroying the surrounding beauty –
Man is experiencing and spreading sorrow daily.

When can we better ourselves?
When can we put an end to all this menace?
When can there be harmony?
We can do all this one day.
Whether that day is nearer or farther, no one knows.
That will be the day we promise ourselves
To experience and spread good deeds and happiness,
And be harmonious like nature,
As we were meant to be.

Bees

In the fields buzzing around,
Honey sweet, it's collecting.
With pollinated flowers in our gardens surrounded,
With pain we cry out from its sting.

Every morning I see;
Even at sunset, it's around.
Going about its work is a bee,
To a hive or flower always bound.

My Wonderful Home – Why All in Shambles?

How pretty is my home,
My planet, my earth.
All the way from dawn to dusk,
The nature remains majestic forever.

The springly tidings behold
The nature waking up in all brightness.
Summer is all hot but cool,
With the trees all together as a shady force.
Monsoon adds some accompaniment,
With nature all wet and fresh.
Décor of rich gold foils all over
With the arrival of autumn in splendour.
Then comes earth's wedding season,
With lovely white wintery flakes all about.

But that's not all.
Home sweet home is just now
Home bitter home.

Springly tidings all forgotten;
It's all about deforestation for a hungry man.
Cool summers not evermore,
When there are no trees about.
Monsoon, I should wait for long;
With no trees, clouds can't shed tears of joy.
Autumn is fiery;
Forest fires burn up the homes.
Earth no longer has a wedding

When wars gobble up the royal, peaceful glory.
How can I call my planet wonderful?

Why can't we live in natural harmony
Why can't there be a natural reality?
It's just for our wonderful home, our earth.

Holiday Wait

Going up the hill
The tired man said he will
Long before the month closed
An adventure he proposed
Pack the bags, he did,
And all anxieties and stress he rid,
For the best holiday fun ever
That he would forget never.

Off the calendar he crossed.
With the excitement caused.
Not another day could he wait'
Nothing would make the holiday
late.

Arrived finally the happy day.
Went he to a land far, far away
For the holiday he booked
With the ideas he cooked.

If There Was No ...

If there was no day,
Darkness would be there everywhere.
If there was no night,
Everything would be heated with hot light.

If there was no summer,
Nothing would be active;
All would be lazy and droopy.
If there was no winter,
We wouldn't dare to step outside
To perspire and get a nice tan.

If there was no control to the winds,
We would be as perfect as
Dry leaves in the wind.
If there was no wind at all,
The nature would be nothing more than
A mere living statue.

If there was no control to nature's forces,
We all would have become history!

Quack, Quack, Quack, Said Mistress Chatterbox

Title inspired by Anne Frank

As I walked along the loch
And saw a raft of ducks,
All said, "Quack, Quack, Quack."
It was then I remembered
That young girl, Annabelle Drack,
Who talked so much –
So fast, so loud,
That she sounded like
The little duckling at the loch.
When I entered the class,
"Quack, Quack, Quack,"
Said Mistress Chatterbox.
Annabelle Drack, here you come.
And then an imposition I would give,
Fit for an incorrigible chatterbox.
But incorrigible was she,
As through the window I would see,
"Quack, Quack, Quack,"
Said Mistress Chatterbox,
As I see those ducks and ducklings
At the beautiful loch.
Annabelle, dear, I still remember that.
"Quack, Quack, Quack,"
Said she, Mistress Chatterbox.

The War

In the beginning,
It was all calm, all peaceful.
Harmony reigned, brotherhood thrived;
Everybody was family.
But as time progressed,
Distance grew.
Humanity began to be torn apart,
And there started war.

Bloodshed, deaths, loss, and suffering.
There upon the sheets,
A kid crying, a mother mourning.
Loss of losses, sorrow of sorrows …

All around rose red,
Horrific as the graveyard.
Wars create such a disastrous scene.

All lose; none win.
The world is in chaos.
Will it end any day?
Will it?

Little Faces, Little Bodies

Out on the streets,
Little faces, little bodies,
Clothed in rags,
Staring with bags
With a message:
Help me, please!

In the ancient café, cleaning every table
In the glass industry, working near the furnace,
Little faces, little bodies.
To read and write, they are not able.
With a sorrowful look that says,
Help me, please!
Everywhere in the world,
Little faces, little bodies.
Nobody cares,
Nobody shares.
I tell you,
Help them, please!

My Yawn

I remember
One fine morning,
I woke up
With a huge wide yawn.
Without much thought,
Ignoring it,
I went on my way.
Again came that dreadful yawn
At the breakfast table.
Oh no!
Will it be a yawny day?

In the school bus,
"Hey, you know what?
That … aaah …"
Oh no!
That dreadful yawn's back.

At school,
Every period, every greeting:
"Good morning, aaah … ma'am."
"All right, maaah … ma'am."
"Wash your face."
"Oh, God! Do you know where you are?"

Teachers strictly commented;
Friends happily laughed.
Oh no!
What a yawny day it was!

My First Sky Adventure

"Passengers, please fasten your seatbelts.
We are now preparing for takeoff.
Please fold your trays and footrests.
Have your seats in the upright position."

My heart was thumping. Then suddenly it was moving.

Then it was sliding up.
Aaaah! My ears closed.
I shut my eyes, pressed my wrist.
So scared was I
That I dreaded an accident.
Then it became still;
I let out a heavy sigh.
I looked out to see a sky so calm,
Filled with huge cotton balls.
Down there was the skyline.
I'm gonna miss it for some time.
Then the hostess patted me for
refreshments.
Wow, that was amazing!
Sky was indeed better than earth,
Way better without schools and textbooks
I looked around to discover …
Lo! Behold! A TV hiding in my armrest.
Not a minute did I waste,
Not an opportunity I missed.
But then back to earth I had to be;
A sad good-bye to say!
Then I decided
Up on the sky is my career.

Woman Power

I met a lady, a CEO,
Who told me a story at a go,
A heart-moving tale.
I thought I'd tell you …

Said she,
"Many years back,
Wiping the floors and washing the clothes,
Not going to school,
Abused and scolded,
Was my mother.
Every day she cried,
Why am I here?
The wife of her employee told my mom
This system, this society,
Is the result of male domination
Where feminism can't flourish.
So my mom strived with her compatriots,
Equalising herself and me
With the so-called guys.

Today, as I recall
That CEO's words,
I wonder
Does woman empowerment really exist?
Is every woman happy?
Is dowry and inequality a thing of past?
Well, I really don't think so.

Still women cry, "We want rights."
Still women cry, "We want to aim big."
Still women cry "Give us a chance."
Still women cry, "We can do it."
Still women cry, "We are capable."
Still women say, "We are equal."

But does anybody hear?
I think the likes of me.
Fight should we,
To get something
That our women folk would
Love to cherish.

If some could be CEOs,
If some could be wealthy,
If some could be awesome –
Why, Why
Can't every woman get a chance?

There shouldn't be dowry.
There shouldn't be inequality.
There shouldn't be restrictions.
There shouldn't be scolding.
All these should be made history.
All these *can* be made history –
If
Woman power can bring an empowerment!

Dreams ... How They Are Made

Don't we young fellas dream as we wish?
Don't we build castles of imaginations far and wide?
Don't we shoot for the stars without thinking of obstacles?
Don't we dream beyond possibilities and the sands of time?
We can because we are just lucky.

Opportunities roll before us;
Careers are multitudinous;
Options out there are endless,
More than the stars out there.

But
Close your eyes,
Sit back,
And reflect ...

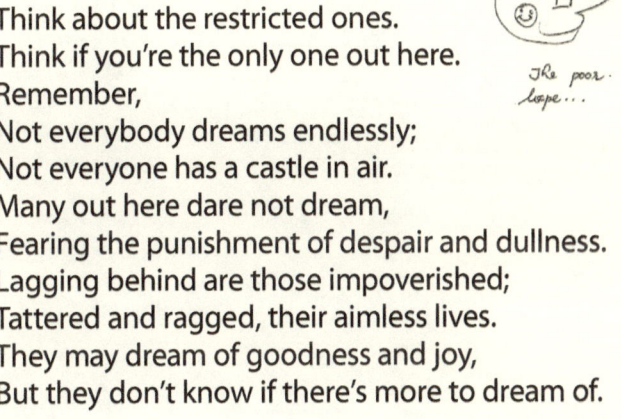

Think about the restricted ones.
Think if you're the only one out here.
Remember,
Not everybody dreams endlessly;
Not everyone has a castle in air.
Many out here dare not dream,
Fearing the punishment of despair and dullness.
Lagging behind are those impoverished;
Tattered and ragged, their aimless lives.
They may dream of goodness and joy,
But they don't know if there's more to dream of.

Such are the dreams,
So discriminating, so different.
When you dream of the most prestigious grad cap,
Or of the highest wages,
There's someone who
Dreams only of a shelter

Or a wholesome meal.
Some dream of a cruise in Queen Mary.
Some dream of a ride in the rickshaw.
Such can be dreams!

Dreams are multitudinous,
Multidimensioned, multifaceted.
But they are what that define you;
They are what keeps you going,
And you are the one who keeps dreams up high.

But,
Only the right place, right time,
Is that which gives the right dream,
Or right to dream –
Not for just you,
But even for those
Who don't realize that a dream exists,
For every child of Mother Earth.

Violet

The strength of royalty you have beneath you,
The color, spreading powerful radiance throughout,
With rainbow standing on you.
The colours of hope on you,
With half the world chasing you.
When heart-throbs are totally on you,
You're so bright, you're so cool.
May not be seen,
But your aura in all of us;
Nobody can forget you.

That Day in Snow

December 20, said the calendar.
The winter break begins, said the school curricular.
The winter collection has arrived, said my favourite store.
And here I come, said Jack Frost.

Cozied up in my room,
Looking out of the window.
Those patterns of ice crystals, snowflakes –
Oh God! What a scene it was!

With fleece sweater and ski boots,
A scarf around my neck,
And a cap on my head,
Ready, set, go:
Heading atop that hill
To ski all the way down.

With my new set of skis and ski poles,
My excitement was hard to beat,
To get atop that hill ski down.

A proud girl was I,
Marching up the hill,
Trudging through the snow.
How lovely was that feeling!

Atop the hill I went,
And screamed down to my sister's army of snowmen,
"Here I come!"

So down the hill I went.
But on the ice I skid off,
And down and down and down I went,
And ended in a nasty accident.
Ouch! It still hurts!

Bygone Writers

Do we ever think
That older writers of the bygone times
Still hold a great position
In our lives?
It is not just the new ones who ought to receive the credit,
But their true inspirers – the ones who have penned down
The true classic literature.
Today's Greene, Rowling, and Kinney
Were the Dickens, Twain, and Bronte of the past.
Who cares now?
But one mustn't forget that these old pens should be thanked
For imparting perfect linguistic knowledge,
Sending information to our brains.
Giving a whole new life
Is what they do for you and me,
With twenty-ounce pages.
Who would ever think
Of repaying these silent teachers?

Charles Dickens:
A serious writer
Who simply taught us
What can be positive and what can be negative
In our irreversible fates.

Mark Twain:
The name might cheer us up,
But that's not all.
Look at the coin's other sides,
And you'll cry.

O Henry,
Master of surprises,
Making literature critical.
Those stories all of us can relish,

And read and read into the night,
At the same time lovable.

The Bronte sisters:
Each has a different story to tell,
From romance to fear.
Dark and complex emotions of life they show.

William Shakespeare:
Pouring out emotions archaicly,
Expressions majestic.
Could be figurative, could be poetic.

Sir Conan Doyle:
My full respect to you for Sherlock Holmes.
Unearthing secrets, holding suspense,
Leaving us spellbound.

Oscar Wilde:
How can his stories be ignored?
Immersing us in
The wonder tales
Of magic and values.

And many more, endlessly on the face of this earth.
A to Z, north or south or east or west,
Many have walked on and off.
But a few have made a difference
Not with a sword,
But a mighty pen.

And so we learn
How powerful all of them
And their like are,
To pen down life and thoughts

That we may cherish,
That may inspire us
That we may tell
For generations to come.

The following articles were first published in *Gulf News*, Dubai, in print and online. Some were under different titles.

1. Man's Greed
2. How Global Warming Rules the World
3. Preserving the Ozone Layer
4. Haunted Experience of an Earthquake
5. My Culture and Your Culture for a Better Tomorrow
6. My Ramadan Memories
7. Human Trafficking
8. Destroying the Spirit of Freedom
9. Rights for Girl Children
10. Eliminating Violence against Women
11. 2014 Nobel Peace Prize
12. A Disagreement
13. Best Fictional Character – Sherlock Holmes
14. Does the Information Age Mean We Are Losing Important Historical Information?
15. Books vs. Movies
16. Freedom of Press
17. Television Is Universal
18. Future of Bullying
19. Live Your Life – Not on Social Media
20. The Cell-Phone Revolution
21. Harsh Eid Climate
22. Anticipating School
23. Spreading Literacy
24. Dubai – Truly Capable
25. Progress Is Not an Illusion
26. India's Space Venture
27. World Post Day
28. International Day of Yoga
29. Breast Cancer Awareness Month
30. Looking Back at a Year of Fear – 2014

www.ingramcontent.com/pod-product-compliance
Lightning Source LLC
Chambersburg PA
CBHW050423290526
45786CB00003B/1386